AMAZON PARROTS

by Paul Paradise

Photography by:

Dr. Herbert R. Axelrod, Joan Balzarini, Michael DeFreitas, Isabelle Francais, Dieter Hoppe, John Manzione, Max Mills, Horst Mueller, K.T. Nemuras, Robert Pearcy, Antonio Perrera, Ronald Smith, Carol Thiem, Vogelpark Walsrode, H. Reinhard, T. Brosset, and Ralph Kaehler.

As popular as parrots are becoming these days, it is no wonder that the Amazon Parrots are topping the list as pet birds kept in the home. They are affectionate, playful, colorful, have amusing personalities, learn to mimic speech, and are available at a fairly modest price. This book, illustrated with over 80 full-color photos, presents sensible, easy-to-follow recommendations about selecting and caring for Amazon Parrots. It concentrates on providing readers with the information they need and want—all given in an interesting and easy-to-read style. Included also is a section on the history of bird keeping, another on taming and training, and an in-depth chapter on the genus *Amazona* with a brief description about each species. If you are considering acquiring one of these lovely creatures, or even if you already have one, this is one book you should not be without.

WHAT ARE QUARTERLIES?

Books, the usual way information of this sort is transmitted, can be too slow. Sometimes by the time a book is written and published, the material contained therein is a year or two old...and no new material has been added during that time. Only a book in a magazine form can bring breaking stories and current information. A magazine is streamlined in production, so we have adopted certain magazine publishing techniques in the creation of this Amazon Parrot Quarterly. Magazines also can be much cheaper than books because they are supported by advertising. To combine these assets into a great publication, we are issuing this Quarterly in both magazine and book format at different prices.

Quarterly

yearBOOKS,INC.

Dr. Herbert R. Axelrod,
Founder & Chairman

Barry Duke
Chief Editor

Linda Lindner
Editor

yearBOOKS are all photo composed, color separated and designed on Scitex equipment in Neptune, N.J. with the following staff:

DIGITAL PRE-PRESS
Patricia Northrup
Supervisor

Robert Onyrscuk
Jose Reyes

COMPUTER ART
Patti Escabi
Sandra Taylor Gale
Candida Moreira
Joanne Muzyka
Francine Shulman

ADVERTISING SALES
Nancy S. Rivadeneira
Advertising Sales Director
Cheryl J. Blyth
Advertising Account Manager
Amy Manning
Advertising Director
Sandra E. Cutillo
Advertising Coordinator

©yearBOOKS, Inc.
1 TFH Plaza
Neptune, N.J. 07753
Completely manufactured in
Neptune, N.J.
USA

Cover design by Sherise Buhagiar

CONTENTS

A History of Bird Keeping

It has been suggested that caged birds were the first true pets that man ever had. This may be correct since caged birds generally served no utilitarian purpose, whereas dogs and cats were used for other purposes such as hunting, pest control and later for food and skins. What is important is that very early in his civilization man went to the trouble to build cages to house birdlife for purposes that were strictly pleasurable and esthetic.

No other animal kept by man at this time served this purpose exclusively.

The Chinese may have been the first bird-keepers, though there is no documented evidence of this. The Chinese did selectively breed pheasants at a time when Europeans had yet to discover the wheel. The first recorded keeping of birds and their exotic wildlife goes back to 1500 BC, when Queen Hatshepsut of Egypt financed an expedition to find animals for her royal

zoo. Many of the animals kept by the royalty of Egypt, such as crocodiles, falcons and hawks, presumably became deities. Parrots were unknown at this time; the Egyptians did not have a hieroglyph for them.

Documents dated as far back as 600 B.C. show that the Chinese were using cormorants (sea birds that dive) for catching fish; this was considerably before Aristotle, who is credited as being the first Western writer about birds. The

Looking at this beautiful Blue-fronted Amazon, it is easy to see why early civilized man began to keep these creatures as pets.

Many royals and nobles kept parrots as pets. Their beauty has attracted them to all types of people including Indians who used their beautiful feathers to decorate their headdresses.

practice of using cormorants still goes on today. Cormorants are very skilled in this due to their long necks. By placing a thread around the neck tight enough so that the cormorants can not swallow their fish, the fisherman is able to fish without using a net or pole. Incidentally, although Aristotle is credited with being the first European to write about birds, Edward Boosey, a well-known ornithologist, claims that approximately one century earlier, in the fifth century BC, a Greek named Ctesias wrote about a bird that talked that came from India. Aristotle wrote about a bird that he named Psittace, which is the basis for the scientific name Psittacidae used for parrots today.

Very elaborate aviaries sprang up in the days of the Roman Empire. At this time the keeping of caged birds, especially talking parrots, was considered a mark of status and the price of such birds often exceeded the price of a slave. One extremely rich Roman, who was one of the pioneers of the mass-produced heating systems used in Roman cities, built a gigantic aviary that matches those produced today. It housed several hundred birds and, instead of metal or wood bars, it had hemp netting.

The introduction of birds, especially parrots, into the Western World can be traced primarily to Alexander the Great, who was well known as a bird fancier. When he reached India, he had the peacocks he saw transported home. He was so enthralled by their beauty that he later issued a decree forbidding the slaughtering of the birds. In the issuing of this decree he may have been influenced by the Indians themselves who elevated peacocks and parrots to a degree of reverence for their beauty and their talking ability. Alexander the Great also introduced the Alexandrine Parrakeet (*Psittacula eupatria*) to Europe. This bird is named appropriately enough for its transporter, and during the days of the Roman Empire was the most popular caged bird. Another bird brought back

The keeping of birds did not become popular until the Industrial Revolution when the building of zoos was instrumental in exhibiting birds to the public and the common person's interest grew.

Bird shows to exhibit the beauty of these creatures began as bird markets. The birds at these shows were based on their quality. Many of the finer specimens went on to be exhibited while those of lesser quality were kept as pets in the home.

by Alexander the Great was the Plumhead Parrakeet (*Psittacula cyanocephala*).

The keeping of birds did not become popular among the lower classes until the Industrial Revolution. The building of modern-size zoos was instrumental in exhibiting birds to the public. At one time the London Zoo, built in 1828, had just about every parrot species. The London Zoo was built after the Vienna Zoo (1752) and the Paris Zoo (1793).

Many traveling shows with trick birds were extremely popular in Great Britain during the early 1800s. One of the most famous was Wombell's Menageries, which had talking parrots and performing canaries in costume. Another, formed by a man named John Austin, gave a performance at Buckingham Palace in 1833 before the young lady who would in a few years become Queen Victoria.

In 1894 the Avicultural Society was founded in England, the first of its kind. Similar bird societies were founded in the United States in 1927 and in Australia in 1928. The rise of bird societies also saw the introduction of a circuit of bird shows. These shows were more accurately bird markets with different classes based on the quality of the stock. Al birds shown at these bird shows were available for purchase afterwards. Today, of course, birds are judged in a variety of categories based solely on esthetic qualities.

INTRODUCTION

There are about 330 species of birds in the family Psittacidae, the parrot family. All 330 species are rightly called parrots, although many of them usually are referred to by other names: macaws, parrotlets, grass parakeets, conures, lories and loikeets, etc. Members of the parrot family are distinguished by their large hooked beaks and their zygodactyl feet. The upper mandible is movable, giving them sufficient force to crack nuts and hard-shelled fruits. The feet of parrots are adapted to forest life and habitation in trees. They have two toes in front and two behind, and most parrots, especially the Amazons, are agile climbers.

The family contains six subfamilies; of these six, the members of the subfamily Psittacinae are the most numerous; they are often referred to as **psittacine** birds, or parrots. In the subfamily Psittacinae are, in addition to the Amazons, parrakeets, conures, parrotlets, lovebirds, grass parrakeets, and other true parrots, like the African Grey Parrot and macaws.

Psittacines are found principally in tropical and subtropical regions. Usually they will be found in low-lying arid forest areas, however, the Andean parrakeet, *Bolborhynchus orbygnesius*, is found in the mountains at an altitude of 15,000 feet.

Psittacines are almost entirely vegetarian in their dietary habits, although in the cage they may accept meat. They are flock birds and in their native countries, are often regarded as pests because of the habit of flying down onto cultivated farmland. Many of the species have been cruelly hunted; several are now extinct. The area comprising the West Indies has been especially hard hit.

Today, many of the Amazon parrots are in danger of becoming extinct, and special emphasis has been placed on endangered species of Amazons in this book. These birds are, of course, no longer available commercially, but the extinction of a species of animal affects us all. The Carolina parrakeet (*Conuropsis carolinensis*) was the only native species of parrot found in the United States. This bird, though once very numerous, went the same way as the passenger pigeon did; the last known specimen died on February 21, 1918 at the Cincinnati Zoo.

Many of the psittacines are well-known talkers. In fact, the most well-known of the talking birds are psittacines. The African Grey Parrot has the reputation of being the world's greatest talking bird. Recently, the *Guinness Book of World Records* gave the title of world champion talking bird to an African Grey named "Prudle," which had a vocabulary of over 1,000 words.

Many of the Amazon parrots are excellent talking birds and come very close to the talking ability of the African Grey. The difference is in the quality of the voice; Amazons have a more nasal voice than African Greys. The Mexican Double Yellow-head and the Yellow-naped Amazon are perhaps the best known talkers among the Amazon parrots.

The Yellow-crowned Amazon Parrot is known to be one of the best talkers of the genus.

The Blue-fronted Amazon is a quite capable talker who is well-liked by bird keepers for he is attractive and rather inexpensive.

THE GENUS AMAZONA

The Amazon parrots belong to the genus *Amazona*, one of the approximately 80 genera in the subfamily Psittacinae. Taxonomists disagree on the exact classification, but most authorities would accept 27 species and over 50 subspecies in the genus Amazona.

Amazons can be found throughout the Central and South American countries and many of the neighboring islands. They are best known of all the New World parrots and, with the exception of the African Grey, are the most widely kept of the true parrots.

Amazons are medium-size parrots and range from 10 to 19 inches in length. They are solid in build and have a basic coloration of green, although red, blue, purple, black and yellow are also to be found.

Amazons have tails that are slightly rounded. The wings are round and very broad, but not very long. Generally, Amazons are

Amazons are medium-sized parrots that range in size from 10 to 19 inches. They are all capable of mimicking the human voice, and for the most part are all very affectionate as well.

expert climbers. They are also excellent talking birds. Amazons are widely kept in the United States. They are popular in Europe, which has a more established bird fancy than in the United States, but in Europe the African Grey is more popular.

Like all other parrots, Amazons are temperamental. They can be highly affectionate, but sometimes they may be very particular about with whom they are affectionate. Sometimes they can be downright nasty to anyone who approaches their cage. They are also noisy birds and will utter shrieks that may keep a bird owner awake throughout the night. Nonetheless, Amazons are intelligent birds and usually will become good, affectionate pets with good training. There are many instances where Amazons have become so tame that they were left completely at liberty, free-flying while their owner is away.

Dr. Matthew M. Vriends, a world-renowned ornithologist who spent some time in Brazil studying Amazons, reports that they fly in large flocks and, to all appearances, mate for life. Vriends also reports that these birds will sleep several hundred in the same tree. Incubation is roughly a month, the same as for the African Grey.

Many of the Amazons change feather coloration as they grow older. This is especially true of the yellow-headed species like the Mexican Double Yellowhead. Amazons have their first molt between eight and ten months of age, and it is with this first molt that they begin to attain their adult coloring.

It is sad to state, but many of the Amazons are on the endangered species list. It is quite possible that, in addition to the birds mentioned in this book, many others may soon be added to the list.

AMAZON PARROT SPECIES

The following list contains the common and taxonomic names of 27 Amazon parrot species.

Yellow-billed or Redthroated Amazon (*A. collaria*)

A pair of Red-lored Amazons displaying affection for one another. Some fanciers consider the yellow, red, and blue facial markings of this Amazon to be among the most attractive in the parrot world.

Amazons, like all other parrots, are quite readily identifiable by virtue of their beak shape and zygodactylous feet.

Scaly-naped or Mercenary Amazon (*A. mercenaria*)

Mealy Amazon (*A. farinosa*)

Vinaceous Amazon (*A. vinacea*)

St. Lucia Amazon (*A. versicolor*)

Red-necked Amazon (*A. arausiaca*)

St. Vincent Amazon (*A. guildingii*)

Imperial Amazon (*A. imperialis*)

The species and subspecies described in this section are currently not on the protected species list. For the sake of clarity, not every subspecies of each species will be listed here, as in most cases the subspecies are very similar to each other. The exceptions are the Double Yellow-headed Amazon (*A. ochrocephala oratrix*) and

Cuban Amazon (*A. leucocephala*)

Hispaniolan or Salle's Amazon (*A. ventralis*)

White-fronted or Spectacled Amazon (*A. albifrons*)

Yellow-lored Amazon (*A. xantholora*)

Black-billed Jamaican Amazon (*A. agilis*)

Puerto Rican or Red-fronted Amazon (*A. vittata*)

Tucuman Amazon (*A. tucumana*)

Red-spectacled or Pretre's Amazon (*A. pretrei*)

Green-cheeked Amazon (*A. viridigenalis*)

Lilac-crowned Amazon (*A. finschi*)

Red-lored or Yellow-cheeked Amazon (*A. autumnalis*)

Red-tailed or Brazilian Green Amazon (*A. brasiliensis*)

Blue-cheeked or Dufresnes' Amazon (*A. dufresniana*)

Festive Amazon (*A. festiva*)

Yellow-faced Amazon (*A. xanthops*)

Yellow-shouldered Amazon (*A. barbadensis*)

Blue-fronted Amazon (*A. aestiva*)

Yellow-crowned Amazon (*A. ochrocephala*)

Orange-winged Amazon (*A. amazonica*)

All Amazons are stocky birds with short, square tails. This St. Vincent Amazon is one of the more rare species in the genus.

the Panama Yellow-fronted Amazon (*A. ochrocephala panamensis*), which are both very popular parrots and deserving of mention. The Double Yellow-head and the Panama Yellow-fronted are both subspecies of the Yellow-Crowned Amazon (*A. ochrocephala*).

The Double Yellow-headed Amazon is very popular for his coloration as well as his ability to mimic the human voice.

Yellow-crowned Amazon (*A. ochrocephala*)

Often called the Single Yellow-headed Amazon, the Yellow-crowned Amazon occupies a wide range, from central Mexico as far south as Peru; it sometimes appears even as far north as southern Texas. It has a great reputation, along with the Double Yellow-headed, as a talking bird. Both birds are

The parrot known as the Yellow-naped Amazon is a form of *Amazona ochrocephala*, the Yellow-crowned Amazon, and bears the subspecific name *auropalliata*.

very popular. In the young the head color is mostly green, with a few patches of yellow. These patches of yellow will become more numerous as the bird grows older and are a distinguishing factor in telling the age of the bird.

Yellow-crowned Amazons, like many other Amazons, utter a variety of shrieks and whistling noises. They are reported to be strong fliers in the wild and capable of flying long distances. In the wild both male and female will sometimes build a nest; this is odd, as most Amazons choose a hollow in a tree and don't build a nest. Incubation of eggs

takes about a month; the usual clutch contains three eggs.

Yellow-crowned Amazons are medium-sized, standing from 14 to 15 inches in length. The crown is yellow and the rest of the head green, although the yellow will gradually spread throughout the head. The cere is black and the beak is dark gray. The iris is orange-colored. The feathers of the nape and hind-neck are green and edged with black. In the young the black edging around the feathers is more pronounced.

Double Yellow-headed Amazon Parrot (*A. ochrocephala oratrix*)

Sometimes called the Mexican Double Yellow-head, the Double Yellow-head stands about 15

Amazona ochrocephala oratix develops its yellow coloration slowly. Youngsters possess Green heads and throats—interspersed yellow feathers slowly spread downward to the neck area.

Domestically bred birds will most likely be hand tame when you purchase them. The Yellow-naped Amazon is one of the more popular species now available on the market.

inches in length. The color of the iris is orange. The bill is more white than that of the Yellow-crowned Amazon. In the young, the head is green speckled with yellow, but as the bird grows older the yellow gradually covers the entire head. This process will continue over 25 years. In the adult the primaries are black and green. The Double Yellow-head is found mainly in Mexico and Belize.

Panama Yellow-fronted Amazon *(A. ochrocephala panamensis)*

Very similar to the Double Yellow-headed Amazon, this subspecies is about 12 inches in length.

The forehead is yellow, with a bluish sheen present; in the young the entire head is green. A patch of red is present at the shoulders. The Panama Yellow-fronted Amazon is found in northern Colombia and Panama. It is often confused with *A. o.auropalliata*, which is sometimes called the Panama Parrot.

Festive Amazon *(A. festiva)*

Sometimes called the Red-backed Amazon, this subspecies is about 14 inches in length. The general plumage is green. The feathers of the neck are faintly edged with black. The crown has a slight bluish tinge. At the

base of the feathers a yellow coloration is present. The iris is yellowish orange.

The Festive Amazon has a geographical distribution that extends throughout eastern Ecuador, eastern Peru and northwestern Brazil. It has a loud, brassy shriek and is found close to the water and in the high treetops that line the Amazon River basin. Oddly enough, even though this is one of the more numerous of the Amazons, it is not often seen in captivity.

Dufresne's Amazon *(A. dufresniana)*

This parrot is rarely seen in captivity and is

Festive Amazon, *Amazona festiva*. Besides eastern Ecuador and northern Peru, the range of this parrot includes a large portion of the Brazilian state of Amazonas.

described as shy in temperament. According to current reports, this parrot is being driven back in its territory in Brazil, where extensive forest-clearing is taking place.

Dufresne's Amazon, also called the Blue-cheeked, has a bluish purple coloration on the cheeks, parts of the neck and ear coverts. The bill is gray, with red at the base of the upper mandible. The general color is dark green. The legs are gray.

Yellow-cheeked Amazon (*A. autumnalis*)

This parrot is found throughout the lowlands of eastern and central Mexico and also to Brazil. It flies in flocks that may number from a few individuals to over a hundred. They are very active during the day and feed on a variety of fruits, nuts and berries.

The Yellow-cheeked is very numerous around the Amazon River basin. Though reported to be noisy in the wild, in captivity they tend to be reserved and suspicious.

The Yellow-cheeked Amazon is 13.5 inches in

Dufresne's Amazon, *Amazona dufresniana*, is similarly uncommon, both in the wild and in captivity.

length. It is often called the Red-lored Amazon or the Scarlet-lored Amazon because of the attractive arrangement of feathers on the crown.

Green-cheeked Amazon (*A. viridigenalis*)

This species is fairly numerous, although found in a limited area in Mexico. Like the Yellow-cheeked, the green-cheeked is found in flocks numbering from few individuals to over a hundred. In flight the birds utter a harsh shriek.

These parrots are great pests and have a reputation for swooping down on cultivated crops, much to the dismay of local farmers. In the wild, these Amazons begin courtship during March. Reportedly, their courtship behavior is accompanied by much shrieking and pecking at each other.

The Green-cheeked is about 13 inches in length. It is often called the Mexican Red-headed Amazon because of the crimson colors on the

All Amazons are stocky birds with short, square tails. This is a Green-cheeked Amazon who is native to eastern Mexico.

forehead, crown and lores. Many people consider this to be the most beautiful of the Amazons. The bill and the iris are yellow. The general plumage is green. In the young the red on the forehead is found only as a patch which gradually expands to cover most of the head. The primaries are blue to black, with a patch of red on the secondaries.

Spectacled Amazon (*A. albifrons*)

This parrot is very common in Mexico and lives in woodlands and dry areas. It feeds on fruits, nuts, berries and leaf buds and is reported to be a pest to farmers; they differ, however, in temperament from other Amazons in being very bold to intruders.

The Spectacled Amazon is also called the White-fronted Amazon, and it is about 14 inches in length. The over-all color of the plumage is green. The forehead and forecrown are white. The crown itself is blue. The feathers of the breast and neck are tinged with black. The size difference between males

The Spectacled Amazon, *A. albifrons*, is smaller than most other Amazon species. Do not let their small size fool you though, they are very bold birds with boisterous personalities.

and females, which is normally slight for parrots, is reported to be very distinct for the Spectacled Amazon.

Orange-winged Amazon (*A. amazonica*)

This parrot occupies a very wide area in northern South America, including parts of Brazil, Venezuela, Colombia and much of Peru. The Orange-winged Amazon is perhaps the most widely available Amazon in Europe. It is an excellent talker and makes a good pet. In the United States the Mexican Double Yellow-head and the Yellow-crowned Amazons are more popular. The smaller size of the Orange-wing makes it easier to house for bird-keepers.

In the wild Orange-winged Amazons are very numerous. Forshaw reports seeing giant bamboo stems so overladen with them that they were bending under their weight. Haverschmidt, a famous bird naturalist, reports them so common in Surinam that the natives kill them for sport because they are pests. In the wild, Orange-winged Amazons feast at the top of trees on

Perhaps the most widely available Amazon in Europe, the Orange-winged Amazon is gaining popularity in the US as well. It is an excellent talker and an easy bird to keep.

a variety of fruits, berries and nuts. They utter a variety of shrill shrieks. Their breeding season begins in February and March.

The Orange-winged is 13 inches in length. The general plumage is green. There is a very attractive display of orange on the wings, interspersed with black, deep blue and green. The crown is yellow. The iris is orange and the legs pale grey. The beak is a yellowish corn color, but darker at the tip.

Blue-fronted Amazon (*A. aestiva*)

The Blue-fronted Amazon is found throughout Brazil and into Argentina. It is

The amount of blue coloration a Blue-fronted Amazon has on its head will vary from bird to bird. Some birds only show slight amounts right above their nostrils, while others have it more interspersed throughout the head.

one of the best known of the Amazons and is very popular in Europe. At one time the popularity of this parrot in Great Britain was second only to that of the African Grey. The first breeding of the Blue-fronted in captivity occurred in 1939. This parrot is an excellent talker.

The Blue-fronted mates during March and often has been observed mating in the same nest year after year. Incubation lasts 29 days. Their food is the same as that of most other Amazons: fruits, berries and nuts. In Brazil they are reported to be a farm pest.

The Blue-fronted is sometimes mistaken for the Orange-winged. The Blue-fronted, however, is bigger, standing 14 to 15 inches in length. The forehead is blue. The general plumage is green. The area around the throat, parts of the cheek and around the eyes are yellowish. The iris is orange, and the bill is grey. The primaries are blue and

The Blue-fronted Amazon was one of the most popular Amazons in Europe. It proves to breed freely, both indoors and out, and is an excellent talker.

black, with a scattering of red.

Cuban Amazon (*A. leucocephala*)

Found in the mountains and the lowlands of Cuba, the Cuban Amazon has become scarce because of the clearing of the land. It is on the list of endangered species proposed by the Washington Convention of 1975. There are very few individuals in captivity.

The Cuban Amazon is very lively. It is a strong flier and very vocal in flight.

In the wild, the Cuban Amazon nests in tree hollows, laying three or

A breeding pair of Cuban Amazons in their wild habitat.

four eggs; the period of incubation is from 25 to 28 days. The young were reported to spend a further 11 weeks in the nest before leaving.

The plumage is mainly green. The Cuban is 13 inches in length. The back part of the neck is blue. The cheeks, lores and parts of the breast are crimson. The ear coverts are dark gray. The feathers of the upper breast are tinged with black.

Salle's Amazon (*A. ventralis*)

Salle's Amazon is often called the San Domingo Amazon. It is rarely seen in captivity and is currently on the list of endangered species compiled by the Washington Convention. It is found on the island of Hispaniola and a few other Caribbean islands.

In the wild these parrots nest in holes in trees. Their breeding season is reported to be variable. They are generally seen in pairs of family groups rather than in large flocks. In the air, they are less strong fliers than other Amazons.

Salle's is a small Amazon about 12 inches in length. The over-all plumage is green. The forehead and forecrown are white. A

Although the Cuban Amazon is a very beautiful bird, it is quite noisy and an indifferent talker. It will do better in an aviary, birdroom, or flight than in very close confinement.

large blackish patch can be observed covering the ear coverts. The beak, legs and feet are flesh-colored. The iris is red. The base of the tail is red. The feathers of the head and mantle are distinctively edged with black.

Yellow-lored Amazon (*A. xantholora*)

This parrot is found in a limited territory around southeastern Mexico and the Yucatan Peninsula. It has been rarely imported and was recently placed on the list of endangered species by the Washington Convention.

The Yellow-lored Amazon is sometimes thought to be a subspecies of *Amazona albifrons*. Both species are markedly similar and in the wild are often found together. Their calls are identical. Early in this century the Yellow-lored was reported to be more numerous, but its numbers are dwindling rapidly. It is found in heavy forest that make detection difficult.

Salle's Amazon, *A. ventralis*, is also known as the Hispaniolan Amazon. This small Amazon, only 12 inches in length, proves to be a most excellent pet and a very proficient talker.

The Lilac-crowned Amazon is so named for the patch of lilac on the top of the head and extending down to the nape.

Amazona finschi, Lilac-crowned or Finch's Amazon. This Amazon inhabits western Mexico, with a range from Durango and Sinaloa southward to Oaxaca. The varied terrain and vegetation of this region afford this parrot a relatively safe harbor.

The general plumage of the Yellow-lored is green; the feathers are edged with black. This is a very small parrot, 10 inches in length. The forehead and crown are white, but the blue coloring of the crown, which is present in the Spectacled Amazon parrot, is absent in the Yellow-lored. The area surrounding the eyes is red. The legs are pale grey. An interesting feature of this parrot is that in the young the forehead is blue, becoming white in the adult.

Lilac-crowned Amazon (*A. finschi*)

This parrot also goes by the name Finch's Amazon. It is not as popular in

Europe as it is in the United States.

The Lilac-crowned is found in the mountainous regions of northwestern Mexico at elevations of about 2,000 feet above sea level. This parrot was more numerous at the turn of the century, when flocks numbering several hundred in number were often observed. In the wild it feeds on an assortment of fruits, berries and nuts. The species has been bred at the San Diego Zoo. The period of incubation was reported to be 28 days, and the chick was hand-raised for a period of three months.

The general plumage of the Lilac-crowned is green, with the feathers edged with black. The forehead is a pale color. The primaries are violet. The iris is orange, the legs greenish grey. The bill is horn-colored. In the young the iris is dark brown. The secondaries are green and blue towards the tip.

Tucuman Amazon (*A. tucumana*)

The Tucuman Amazon is rarely seen and today occupies a small area in southeastern Bolivia. It has been placed on the endangered species list compiled by the Washington Convention of 1975.

The length of the Tucuman is 13 inches. The general plumage is green, with the feathers strongly tinged with black. The

A promising pair of Tucuman Amazons, *Amazona tucumana*. The courting ritual in parrots is always a delight to witness, one of the many advantages to owning and keeping a breeding pair of parrots.

forehead is red. The primaries are green, becoming blue towards the tip. The iris is orange-yellow, and the legs are a pale greyish pink.

Red-spectacled Amazon (*A. pretrei*)

This is a rare parrot in captivity and was placed on the Washington Convention list of endangered birds. Apparently, the Red-spectacled was more common in the early part of the century, but widespread clearance of forest land has been largely responsible for its dwindling numbers. Foreshaw, however, as recently as 1971, reported that they are quite plentiful in their limited territory in southeastern Brazil. Foreshaw reported seeing over a thousand of them in one particular location, but he warns that with the continuing depletion of their natural habitat they will rapidly dwindle in number as have many of the other Amazons.

The Red-spectacled is 13 inches in length. Its forehead is red, as is the area surrounding the eyes and parts of the shoulders. The iris is yellow, and the bill is horn-colored. Parts of the wing feathers are also red. This parrot is very similar to the Tucuman Amazon; they can be distinguished from each other by a patch of red at the wing tips that is found on the Red-spectacled.

In the wild, the Tucuman Amazon inhabits alder forests, however, the extensive clearing of the evergreen forests in recent decades has markedly reduced the habitat of this and most other Amazons that live there.

Red-tailed Amazon (*A. brasiliensis*)

The Red-tailed is also called the Brazilian Green Amazon. It is found in a small area in southern Brazil. It once occupied a wider territory, but extensive deforestation in that country has considerably diminished its territory. It has rarely been kept in captivity. In the wild, it is often seen in the company of the Red-spectacled Amazon (*A. pretrei*).

The general plumage is green. The top of the head is pinkish. The cheeks, throat and upper breast are greyish with blue interspersed. The primaries are black and deep blue. The tail has a band of yellow and a band of red. The iris is brown, and the legs are grey.

Vinaceous Amazon, *Amazona vinacea* is found in southeastern Brazil, northeastern Argentina and southeastern Paraguay. The name Vinaceous refers to the wine-colored chest and throat coloration.

Vinaceous Amazon (*A. vinacea*)

The Vinaceous Amazon is not often seen in captivity; it was placed on the endangered species list proposed by the Washington Convention. The main appearance of the species until this time has been in Europe, where it has a reputation as a colorful Amazon parrot and also a good aviary bird. Although not much has been written about it, the Vinaceous is reported to be a very gentle bird, which is not the usual case as far as parrots go. It has been bred in captivity many times. The eggs are oval and smooth. It is found in southeastern Brazil.

The Vinaceous is 14 inches in length. Its overall plumage is green. The forehead and lores are red. The iris is red, and the legs pale grey. The upper regions of the breast and abdomen are violet, sometimes bluish-green. The primaries are black and blue.

Mercenary Amazon (*A. mercenaria*)

The Mercenary Amazon parrot occupies a narrow but extensive coastal area beginning near Venezuela and Colombia and extending south through Bolivia, Peru and Chile. This parrot is very rare, and little information has been published about it. It is considered to be an endangered species.

The Mercenary Amazon is a shy bird that occupies hilly, mountainous regions. The natives in the regions in which it lives are rarely able to find its nesting spots. Its call and its nesting habits have thus far not been recorded.

The general plumage is green. The Mercenary Amazon is also called the Scaly-naped Amazon and is identified by a yellowish patch on the crown. The iris is red. The legs and the bill are grey. The wings, although green, are laced with red and have black edging.

Yellow-faced Amazon (*A. xanthops*)

The Yellow-faced Amazon, also called the Yellow-bellied Amazon, is found mainly in eastern Brazil. It was reported to be more numerous at the turn of the century, but little has been recorded about its habits. Its call is undescribed.

Yellow-faced Amazon, *Amazona xanthops*. Only meager information is available on this Amazon's life in the wild. The often very inaccessible terrain makes tracking down and observing this species very difficult.

The over-all plumage is green; some feathers on the nape and hind-neck are edged with dark green and narrowly topped with black. The iris is yellow. The legs are pale grey. The bill is horn-colored. The primaries and secondaries are edged with a greenish yellow.

ENDANGERED AMAZON SPECIES

From the foregoing species descriptions you can see that many species are already quite scarce, and that many are on the 1975 Washington Convention's list of endangered species. The species in this section, in addition to being on the Washington Convention's list, are protected species in their own country and as such have not been available to the public eye for quite some time. It is hoped that a time will come when these species, many of which were numerous at one time, will again become plentiful enough that they can be bought commercially or be on display in zoos across the world.

Puerto Rican Amazon (*A. vittata*)

The Yellow-shouldered Amazon, *Amazona barbadensis*, inhabits savannah-like coastal regions of Venezuela.

St. Vincent Amazon, *Amazona guildingii*. The quickly vanishing tropical uplands of the small Caribbean island of Saint Vincent serve as the last refuge for this rare, endangered Amazon parrot.

The Puerto Rican Amazon, also called the Red-fronted Amazon, is a small and well proportioned parrot. It is about 12 inches long and is found only in Puerto Rico. Forshaw says that a subspecies of *A. vittata* used to exist on a nearby island but is now extinct. The last specimens of this subspecies were collected in 1899.

Dr. Russ, author of *The Speaking Parrot*, reports that the Puerto Rican Amazon used to be among the most plentiful of the imported species. Its decline was very rapid at the turn of the century. Reasons for its decline are numerous; hunting for sport, killing as a farm pest and nest-robbing for feathers. Additionally, vast deforestation has helped deplete its numbers. Recently 28,000 acres in the mountain areas of eastern Puerto Rico were set aside as a preserve for the bird.

Surveys made between 1953 and 1956 estimated the number of wild Puerto Rican Amazons as 200; surveys in 1956 estimated the number at 50. This number was changed to 30 in 1968, and today only 22 are thought to remain. This parrot is on the Washington Convention's endangered list.

The main color of the Puerto Rican Amazon is green, with a narrow band of red on the forehead. Flecks of red also cover the ear-coverts and cheeks. The outer webs of the flight and tail feathers are blue. The tip of the tail is yellow, which is also the color of the bill and the iris.

Senseless predation is not the sole cause for the decline of the Puerto Rican Amazon. During World War II, the cutting down of old Colorado trees contributed to the greatly decreasing numbers of this parrot. Scientists have since learned that

this parrot will not nest in any other tree. The Puerto Rican is also vulnerable to attacks by rats and by a bird called the Pearly-eyed Thrasher (*Margarops fuscatus*), which, due to lack of trees on the

island, has more or less usurped those of the Puerto Ricans. The thrasher is a small but vicious bird, and one biologist reported killing 26 of them which were attempting to drive a single Puerto Rican Amazon from its nest.

Yellow-shouldered Amazon Parrot (*A. barbadensis*)

The scientific name for the Yellow-shouldered is based on a mistake, since the wold *barbadensis* translates to "of Barbados" and these parrots are not found on Barbados at all. They are found almost exclusively on the island of Aruba, situated just off the coast of Venezuela.

At the turn of the century, this species was reported as very numerous in the wild, though extremely shy and not easily caught due to their limited territory. The bird's rapid demise is linked to the expansion of the oil-refinery business in Venezuela. In 1955, the Yellow-shouldered was claimed to be extinct, but two specimens were observed in 1957. Its reduction in numbers throughout 1930 to 1940 was quite rapid, and by 1948 only a few breeding pairs were

Although the Yellow-shouldered Amazon is not a common bird in captivity, many keepers have done quite well in breeding and rearing them.

thought to be left in existence. This parrot is on the Washington Convention's list of endangered species.

The Yellow-shouldered is very similar to the Mexican Double Yellow-head (*A. ochrocephala oratrix*). It is 13 inches in length. The forehead and lores are a yellowish white. The crown, cheeks and ear-coverts are yellow. The flight feathers are quite dark, ranging from a dark blue to almost black. The eye is a dark orange and the beak is light horn color. The shoulders are a bright yellow.

Red-necked Amazon, *Amazona arausiaca*, a very attractive and very threatened parrot of Dominica, West Indies.

If you are lucky enough to have one of these gems, the Red-necked Amazon makes an extremely playful and charming pet.

Imperial Amazon Parrot (*A. imperialis*)

The Imperial Amazon parrot is the largest species of the genus *Amazona*. It is 19 to 20 inches in length. From its name alone one would guess that it is a beautiful bird; indeed, the Duke of Bedford, who kept many of the Amazons, called it "the emperor of all true parrots." The head, neck, breast and abdomen are a purplish blue, with black edges to the feathers. The feathers of the crown and the back of the neck are edged with dark green. The primaries and secondaries are dull purple, with green

St. Vincent Amazon Parrot (*A. guildingii*)

This species is found only on the island of St. Vincent in the Lesser Antilles. This parrot has always been rare. A specimen was first exhibited in the London Zoo in 1874. They are reported to be good talkers although not as good as other Amazons like the Mexican Double Yellow-head.

Although not on the Washington Convention's list of endangered species, the St. Vincent Amazon is in imminent danger of extinction. Under 500 of the birds are believed to be alive on the 130 square-mile island of St. Vincent. Those parrots that have been transferred to zoos have not done well either, and all but three or four have died. The only successful captive breeding to date of a pair of St. Vincent Amazons was at the Houston Zoo early in the 1970's.

In the late 1800's the St. Vincent was one of the most popular of the Amazons because of its size and coloration, which are said to be second only to those of the Imperial Amazon. The demise of the St. Vincent was caused by a number of factors. One was a severe hurricane in 1898 that left the surrounding rivers and coastal areas flooded. A volcanic eruption followed immediately afterward, which killed off more parrots as well as destroyed their nesting sites. St. Vincent Amazons are slow breeders and never fully recovered from these calamities.

The St. Vincent Amazon is also called Guilding's Amazon Parrot. It is 16 to 18 inches in length. The forehead, front of the crown, as well as the area round the eyes, are white. The feathers of the crown are tipped with lilac, as are the cheeks and ear coverts. The iris is orange and the bill is corn-colored. The upper tail coverts are brown. The feathers of the neck are blue and the feathers of the upper breast are brown.

Saint Vincent Amazon, *Amazona guildingii*. It is probably safe to say that the Saint Vincent Amazon can no longer be found in the aviaries of bird keepers. The zoos that are fortunate to have these birds must act quickly to repopulate the species.

Saint Vincent Amazon, *Amazona guildingii*. The wild numbers of this very attractive parrot are estimated to be in the low hundreds. If the Saint Vincent Amazon is to be saved from extinction, man must take immediate action.

SELECTING AND TRAINING

PARROTS IN THE WILD

People often forget that the parrot, in contrast to the canary or the budgerigar, is basically a wild bird. It is distrustful of man. Although most parrots are eventually tamed, parrots are temperamental. They form intimate likes and dislikes that can be very difficult to change. That is why only one person should be the trainer. Another thing that is important is that only a young bird, one that has not yet formed a personality, should be trained.

Before this century, a prospective bird-owner was at a disadvantage. For one thing, the bird he bought was usually an older bird (in commercial trade a bird that is much over a year old is considered to be "old"). The older bird was chosen because it had a better chance of survival due to the long shipment time. Also, when a young bird was shipped it was often an older bird by the time it was offered for sale. Not only were these parrots difficult to train, but the bird-owner was given little instruction on how to properly train his bird. Some of the taming techniques used were absolutely useless. One technique was to hit the

bird if it refused to talk. This did more damage than the trainer could wish because a bird has an instinctual fear of a man's hand. Another trick, in common use, was cutting the bird's tongue in the hopes of increasing its possible vocabulary. This will do nothing.

teach his new parrot to talk in a week. Properly training a bird takes many months, and you should not be discouraged if it takes six months or longer. The thing to remember is that you are taming an essentially wild bird and, above all else, will have to gain its confidence.

Amazons can be startled very easily. It is therefore important that you keep your hand where your bird can see it at all times. Never try to pet your Amazon from the back of the head, but rather begin from the front.

Another method, still practiced today, is the "shotgun" method where the owner attempts to

BUYING A PARROT

The first requirement in purchasing a parrot is to be familiar with the size and coloration of the parrot itself. Unfortunately, many of the common names for parrots are confusing and there are unscrupulous people willing to take advantage of people's gullibility. One good example is with the African Grey, which is a very popular parrot. Sometimes the African Grey is mistaken for the Australian Roseate Cockatoo or Galah (*Eolophus roseicapilla*). Although I have never seen this cockatoo being passed off as an African Grey, I have read that it is sometimes sold under the name of the Australian Grey Parrot. There is no such bird, and the prospective bird-owner should be aware of this discrepancy since the prices of the two birds are different. Both of these birds are about the same size and both are grey and have pink colors on the breast. This is not to say that the Galah Cockatoo is not an excellent aviary bird—in fact, of all the cockatoos kept in captivity it may well be the most popular. However, the Galah Cockatoo is not as gifted a talker as the African Grey and is much more noisy. This example is not mentioned to discourage prospective bird-owners, but just to show that either the advice of another bird-owner should be utilized or the birds should be purchased only from a

In the wild, Amazons naturally gnaw on leaves, twigs and bark from non-toxic plants and trees.

reputable pet shop or avairist.

The next requirement after you have found the parrot you desire is to determine the physical soundness of the bird. The parrot should not be missing any toes, nor should there by any evidence of mites on him. The nostrils should be clean and dry, without a watery discharge. The birds should have an intelligent look and be interested in

what is going on. A bird that keeps its eyes closed or has discharge coming from the eyes may be sick. Since most birds have not yet molted, their feathers will look dry and lack sheen. A bird that is sick will slouch on its perch with its feathers puffed up; the bird does this to retain body heat.

Interestingly enough, feather condition has little to do with the purchasing of a bird. According to Bob

Novak of Novak's Aviaries, Long Island, the wing feathers and tail feathers are often pulled out by local natives, who later sell them. Also, the wings may be clipped for ease of shipping. Neither of these conditions is critical since the bird will get a new set of feathers when it molts. A bird with its wings clipped may look awkward because it will not be able to balance itself properly. If there is any question, ask the owner or spread the bird's wings yourself.

In an article entitled "Taming Your Parrot" by Terry Clymire in the June-July 1978 issue of *Bird World, American Aviculturists Gazette,* the author says that the pet shop owner may guarantee the health of the birds he sells. This may not be a widespread practice, but according to Clymire, under the terms of the agreement, if the owner takes his bird to a veterinarian, who in turn finds the bird unfit, it may be returned to the pet shop owner for a refund.

ACCLIMATIZATION

Acclimatization of a bird like the parrot is critical only if the bird-owner later transfers the bird to an aviary. All parrots are quarantined after importation, and most bird importers are very meticulous in their examination of potentially sick birds. Thus, the parrot purchased in a pet shop is usually in very good health.

All Amazons are natural climbers and should therefore be permitted to do so freely. Ladders and climbing frames can be purchased from your local pet store and are very much enjoyed by these birds.

If a parrot is to be transferred to an aviary, then it should not be introduced for a period of two weeks. This is always a good precaution before introducing it into an aviary full of birds. Also, the bird-keeper will want to gain some familiarity with the bird.

For the parrot that is to be kept alone in a cage, the bird-owner should be sure that the cage is ready for it when it arrives home. The cage should be large enough to accommodate the bird, with space above its head, and at a minimum wide enough for it to flap its wings. The cage should be in an elevated position, free from drafts, and with a room

Once your Amazon is hand tame he will enjoy having his head and neck scratched.

A wooden climbing frame may quickly be destroyed by your Amazon Parrot's beak. Chewing and climbing are the two things Amazons enjoy most.

Your Amazon parrot will occasionally test the surface he wishes to step on with his beak. Do not pull away when he does this, or else he may bite down and inflict pain.

temperature between 68 and 75°F. Water, seed, grit and perhaps a piece of fruit should be placed inside.

Amazons that are somewhat tame may not step onto your hand on their own accord. You may have to lift the bird off by its feet in order to get him down.

The cage should be covered for the first day.

TRAINING

The first requirement of training is to make sure that other family members do not interfere in the process. Nothing makes a bird more skittish than a cluster of unfamiliar faces and sounds. Birds are much more attuned to quick, sudden movements than is generally suspected.

The first step is to open the cage door and stick the hand inside. The parrot may bite or peck at first, since it has an instinctive fear of a man's hand. The hand should never be inserted with the fingers extended, but with the palm face downward. If the bird will not perch the first few times do not be alarmed; moreover, do not force it or tease it. There are cases of a parrot becoming forever suspicious of an individual who teased it. This first lesson should last no more than 15 or 20 minutes a day. The object is to show the bird that the hand is friendly, something that will need much patience.

The bird-owner will sense when he is making progress. The next step is to get the bird to perch on the hand, and eventually to perch on the hand and be taken outside of its cage. Use a net if the bird flies away. Trying to catch a bird by hand may be disastrous. Parrots are big and bulky and cannot be held like a budgie or

You will find it easy to train your Amazon parrot when you offer him his favorite seed as a reward for a job well done.

This Mexican Red-Headed Amazon is a fine example of what a healthy bird looks like. It has good feather condition, a well-aligned beak, clear eyes, no discharge from the nostrils, and good weight to its body.

The best place to train a new Amazon is in a corner of a room where it cannot get away from you. A bird trained here will have no distractions or hiding places that it can run to for cover.

TEACHING TO TALK

Parrots that have been well-trained turn out to be better talkers. Amazons will learn new words all of their lives and will not slow with age. The only real impediment in teaching a bird to talk is the introduction of other birds. If other birds are introduced they become more interested in each other than in learning to talk.

Both male and female Amazons are good talkers. Tales of birds that can recite long phrases and poetry are not exaggerations. Birds, however, do not speak, they mimic. The first few lessons, like the training lessons, should be short, no more than 20 minutes at first. Pronuciation and voice inflection should be

canary. Using a net is much simpler and reduces the risk of damaging the bird's wings. A butterfly net will suffice, or a special net can be bought at a pet store. Those purchased in pet stores come in different size meshes and are made of nylon.

If a bird seems reluctant to perch on either a gloved or bare hand, then the owner might try using a wooden perch. The parrot may accept this more readily than the hand. Hold the perch under the bird's breast and gently push it under the bird so that it will be forced to step onto it. The parrot will move away several times, but gradually it can be induced to perch on this and later on the hand.

After a bird has learned to perch, it should be taken for a tour of the house. This is to show the bird that its cage is not its only home. If training was done consistently and the bird's confidence gained, it can be placed on a perch that doesn't have a wire around it. Many parrots live completely at liberty, and all bird-owners should have this goal in mind when training.

If you like talking to your bird and watching it learn new words, you can use modern training tools to effectively expedite the process. Have fun conversing with your feathered friend. Call 1-888-605-TALK for a store near you. Photo courtesy of Wordy Birdy Products.

regulated so as not to confuse the bird.

The first word to be learned should be short, no more than two syllables. The word should be repeated, with a short pause between each recital. The pause is so the bird will not continually repeat the phrase after it learns it. Do not be surprised if the bird slurs or mispronounces the word on its first try. Keep repeating the word until the bird's pronunciation improves. Reward the bird if it does well.

While the time taken may vary considerably, the

A perch away from your bird's cage that your Amazon can sit upon will be well liked by your Amazon.

The Yellow-naped Amazon is known for his exceptional talking ability. This bird is very proficient in picking up words, phrases and even songs.

main thing is not to get discouraged. I have read of one bird-owner who needed eight months to teach his pet parrot its name.

Getting the bird to respond to a particular phrase is difficult, but not impossible. The bird must be taught a conditioned response; connecting a particular phrase with a particular action or phrase on the part of the owner. One method is to approach the cage, stop and say the phrase, "Fine, thanks," every time the owner approaches the cage. The owner then says, "How are you?' when he approaches the cage to which the bird answers "Fine, thanks," gradually the bird will connect the coming of the owner to the cage and the

phrase "How are you?" with the response "Fine, thanks."

TOYS

Toys are really a much needed amusement in the cage, especially for Amazons. Parrots are prone to nervousness and never completely adjust to cage life. The addition of toys provides a diversion for the bird for whom nervousness becomes a neurotic habit sometimes called "displacement preening." Displacement preening is a condition where the bird begins to scratch its head and pick out its feathers from all over its body to the point of actual injury. The only cure is to provide some diversion.

The Yellow-crowned Amazon develops its yellow coloration slowly. Youngsters possess green heads and throats.

YOUR AMAZON PARROT'S DIET

BASIC FOOD REQUIRE-MENTS

Parrot owners are at an advantage over budgie and canary owners because parrots will eat a variety of foods besides their basic seed mixtures. Parrots will eat corn, a variety of fruits and vegetables, many types of seeds, bread, peanuts and even meat. Most parrots are fussy eaters, but this should not discourage the owner from experimenting.

The basic requirements for a bird are seed, water, cuttlebone and grit. The seed is most important since the bird derives most of its nourishment from this source.

Because of their size, Amazons prefer hefty amounts of larger seed, especially peanuts and sunflower seeds, in their diet.

Canary Seed

Canary seed comes from canary grass (*Phalaris canariensis*) and, although it grows in wild form, is cultivated in central and southern Europe. It grows to a height of two feet and

In the wild, the social behavior of Amazons is often contingent on the environment and availability of foods—a constant food source deters an individual species' need to wander from area to area.

has bluish leaves. The leaves are elongate like normal grass; the seed heads are oval or in panicles (loosely branched flower clusters).

With sufficient sunlight the panicles ripen and when collected are thoroughly dried to prevent moldiness. The term Spanish is used to describe top-quality seed.

Good seed is fairly large, uniform in size and pale yellow in color. The skin is clean and bright, and when the outer shell is dirty or dull or the inner kernel very light or very dark, then the seed is not of top quality. It may have been badly harvested, insufficiently dried or picked before it was completely ripened.

Canary seed contains the following nutrients: water (13.5%), protein (13.5%), fats and oils (4.9%), starch and other carbohydrates (51.6%) and ash and mineral elements (2.1%).

Millet Seed

Millet is used basically as a filler mixed with other seeds, principally canary. Another use of millet is for exercising the stomach muscles because it has tough fibers. For overweight or underexercised birds, millet is usually given in bigger doses.

Your Amazon's diet should be based on the type of thoroughly researched and quality-tested foods that are available to birdkeepers today; such foods visibly improve color and vitality. Ask your veterinarian about specialty care diets. Call 888-286-2473 for a pet dealer nearest you. Photo courtesy of Roudybush, Inc.

lories and lorikeets. Other species of millet are Hungarian millet (*Panicum germanicum*) and Indian millet (*Panicum miliare*).

The nutrient composition of millet is carbohydrate (61.5%), fats and oils (5%) protein (15%), water (13%) and ash and mineral elements (1.6%).

OIL SEEDS

Oil seeds are rich in amino acids, particularly the amino acid lysine, which the non-oil seeds do not have. Since oil seeds are fattening, they are fed only on a weekly basis, either separately or mixed with the regular seed. Common oil seeds used are niger, rape and linseed.

Fruits and vegetables should be offered to your Amazon on a daily basis. Why not hang an assortment of these from a chain to give your bird his treat in a fun way.

Millet is the common name for a wide variety of plants belonging to the genus *Panicum*. Like canary, millet is a grass, of which the most widely used is the plant growing in the tropical arid regions of Africa and the Middle East. This is called white millet (*Panicum miliaceum*). White millet grows to a height of four feet. Its introduction into Europe has resulted in many different varieties, such as black, red, gray and brownish seed.

Another common species of millet is spray millet (*Panicum italicum*), grown in France and Italy. This seed is yellow and smaller than white millet. Spray millet is reserved for smaller birds like finches,

Dried fruits and other favored foods like monkey biscuits will prove to be a favored "extra" in your Amazon's diet. Feed this and all supplemental food items in addition to a basic seed diet.

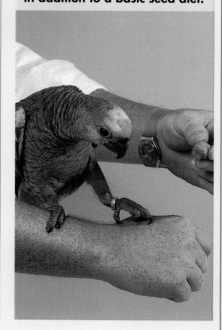

Peanuts make up an important part of most parrots' menu, though not as vital a component to the diet as sunflower seeds.

Like all animals, birds love special treats. Owners can feel especially good knowing they're giving their pet birds something that tastes good and is good for them. Photo courtesy of Kaytee Products, Inc.

Niger Seed

Niger seed is grown in northern India and was once used for lamp oil because of its high oil content. Niger seed (*Guizotia abyssinica*) is closely related to sunflower seed.

Niger seed contains close to 25% oil. When refined, the oil turns from a brown to a pale yellow color. The better the quality of seed the more black and shiny is the husk. Some breeders do not use this seed or only feed it during the breeding season. The reason for this is that niger is more prone than the other oil seeds to turn rancid. Niger seed is a small, long, thin seed and is often squashed during commercial transportation. This spoils the quality of the oil. In commercial mixtures niger is mixed with other oil seeds like rape and linseed.

The nutrient content of niger is water (8.4%), protein (17.5%), fats and oils (32.7%), starches and other carbohydrates (15.3%) and ash and trace elements (7.0%).

Rape Seed

Rape seed is from a species of cabbage. The types usually encountered are the English and the German. Both are members of the genus *Brassica*, but the German is the one used most often in commercial mixtures. Good rape seed is red to purplish brown in color. Like niger it is small, but is round and less prone than niger to turn rancid during storage.

The nutrient content of rape seed is water (11.5%), protein (19.4%), fats and oils (40.5%), starches and other carbohydrates (10.2%) and ash and mineral matters (3.9%). Rape has an unusually high quantity of phosphoric acids, almost 50 percent of it is ash and mineral content.

Linseed

Linseed (*Linum usitatisssimum*) comes from the flax plant. Flax reaches about two feet in height. The leaves are narrow and usually attain an inch in length. The flowers are blue. Linseed is also fed to race horses along with oats for its oil content. Like all of the oil seeds, linseed must be of

Birds have unique dietary needs that must be met by certain seeds and other foods. To be sure your bird is getting what it needs, it is important to feed a diet you can be sure has been created specifically for it by teams of experts. Photo courtesy of Kaytee Products, Inc.

Good nutrition is important. Birds can live for years on a bad diet, but in the long run their lives are shortened and their health suffers. Variety is always of benefit, not only nutritionally but mentally.

GREENS

Greens provide vitamins, principally vitamin A for the eyes. They are also important as a source of pigment for keeping up the feather color. For some parrots which drink very little, like the African Grey, the addition of greens serves as an additional source of moisture.

Greens are the easiest of the bird's nutritional requirements to supply since they can be grown at home or purchased in a supermarket. Spinach, endive, chickweed and lettuce are commonly eaten by Amazons. Lettuce contains more nutritional value than is usually ascribed to it.

FRUITS

Amazons will eat a variety of fruits:oranges, apples, melons, etc. The owner needs to remember that a bird's throat is not as large as its mouth. Oranges and apples should be sliced and hung at the side of the cage.

COD-LIVER OIL AND WHEAT GERM OIL

Cod-liver and wheat germ oils are often used by aviary owners as an added source of nutrients. Neither is a must, but because they are oils they might be given as an added source of amino acids. They are not to be mixed into the grit or seed mixture as they will turn rancid. They should be mixed in a special seed mix that is to be fed to the bird on the day mixed. They might also be used when the birds reach the breeding season to help prevent egg-binding.

PELLET DIETS

Relatively new on today's market are pelleted diets

As studies in avian nutrition advance, pet birds benefit from increased nutritional and structural variety in their diets. See how your bird enjoys the tastes and textures of modern bird foods. Photo courtesy of Sun Seed Company.

Consider all of an Amazon's characteristics before you bring one home. Remember, these birds require ample time away from their cage and can be quite destructive with their beaks.

other types of foods that are high in egg content. This is particularly important during the breeding season, even if you are not breeding your birds because hormonal changes are still taking place in non-breeding birds. Hard boiled egg, or bread with a high egg content will be relished by most Amazons. Stale rolls or white bread that has been soaked in milk will also be very welcome additions to the diet, and prove to be beneficial supplementary foods.

The importance of offering your pet Amazon as wide and as varied diet as possible cannot be stressed enough. Big parrots, such as the Amazons, are often given, and thrive well on, those foods that are normally intended for

for birds. Not only do these diets contain all of a bird's nutrients in a completely pelleted form, they are also beneficial because they waste a lot less. With pellets, it is not necessary to change that which is offered on a daily basis, only replenishment is needed. Many veterinarians and breeders believe that pelleted diets are the only way to ensure proper nutrient intake. While many of these diets claim to be nutritionally balanced

and complete, this can only be proven by the health of a bird that eats and thrives on such a diet. If your Amazon seems to consume a small amount of pellets, it would be wise to check with your veterinarian about feeding a half seed and half pellet diet so that the health of your feathered friend does not suffer.

OTHER FOODS

In addition to seeds, fruits, and pellets, Amazon parrots should be offered

Hand-tame Amazons truly are affectionate pets. They are very intelligent birds that love to be cuddled and loved by their owners.

human consumption—table food. There is nothing wrong with giving parrots moderate amounts of this in addition to their regular diet, providing the food agrees with them. Under no circumstances, however, should they receive very salty or otherwise highly spiced foods.

GNAWING

As parrots are characterized by having a pronounced urge to gnaw, it is necessary to supply them with fresh twigs that will enable them to exercise their beak in this way. The thickness of the twigs will, of course, depend on the species of parrot. Suitable twigs include those from all fruit trees except cherry, and those from elderberry, willow, hazelnut, or pine.

Many household plants are toxic to your bird if ingested. Always be certain to watch your bird during the time he spends away from his cage.

AVIARY KEEPING

The aviary is a compound structure that has two sections: the shelter or birdhouse and the flight. The flight is used for exercise. It is a wire enclosure that is usually four or five times larger than the birdhouse. There is a doorway or entrance connecting the two so the birds can fly from the birdhouse into the flight.

The prime considerations in buying or building an aviary are the space available, and the number of birds to be housed. As to the selection of the birds, the aviarist should always be aware that birds are territorial and some birds are mean towards smaller birds. Also, if the birds are to be bred, then breeding pairs should never occupy the same area or they will fight. The rule for breeding parrots is one pair or three pairs or more, but never two pairs.

the aviary without worrying about warping or muddying the floor.

The roof of the birdhouse is usually made of shingles, sheet metal or tile. Ventilating ducts are also drilled near the roof, which

Some parrots are more apt to mimic words and phrases than others. If this is an important attribute for your new pet to have, to be sure to purchase a species noted for its talking ability.

The size aviary that you choose for an Amazon parrot must be large enough so that the inhabitants can spread their wings and fly back and forth with ease.

The floor of both the birdhouse and the flight is made from either cement or hardwood. Bare earth can be used but, in additon to harboring parasites, it may have to be dug over every few months, limed and returfed. Cement allows the bird-owner to hose down is slanted for rainfall. The ducts are wirecovered to prevent the birds from getting out and predators from getting in. Predation is a major problem with aviaries since mice, weasels, raccoons and stray cats are very adept to crawling under wire or biting through it. One bad night has wiped out more than one aviarist.

Heating may be a radiator or an electric heater. This should be placed in the birdhouse and great care should be taken in the matter of fire safety. The inside of the birdhouse usually has a great deal of hay or foliage for nest-building or for the birds to play with. A fire inside a birdhouse would be a great tragedy.

Netting or wire for the aviary is determined by the weight and size of mesh. The smallest mesh for budgies is one-half to three-quarters of an inch mesh. Usually one-inch mesh is used for parrots. This will not keep mice out, but being larger and stronger, will present an obstacle to weasels and raccoons. Usually mesh is painted so the birds will be better able to distinguish it. Lead-free paint, the kind used to paint baby furniture, is the best. As already mentioned, Amazons are chewers and would swallow any chips of paint they could chew away.

Aviary netting and hardware cloth can be ordered through a hardware dealer. Hardware cloth is more expensive than aviary netting but is less brittle.

Most flight sections are made of wire with wooden frames. Sometimes several flight sections are attached

Front view of the Red-lored Amazon in which the blue coloration of the head is clearly visible.

to one central birdhouse. A good size of flight for parrots is from 15 to 20 feet, with a height of eight feet. Perches or roosts are placed near the ceiling, since not only do birds like to roost in elevated positions, but when the bird-owner enters he will not have to distract the birds.

The birdhouse is often a converted shed, garage or greenhouse. If you are not a handyman, several types of indoor birdhouses can be purchased, with or without a shelter attached. These indoor birdhouses

A bird's good health, or lack there of, will show in its plumage and over-all body stance.

are usually made of wood with wire to keep the birds from flying away. Sometimes rollers are on the bottom for ease of movement. The small size of these birdhouses prohibits the keeping of more than a single parrot or a breeding pair.

Some bird breeders insist on a small flight section, say of under four feet in length. These breeders have a multitude of young fledglings at any time and, since these birds are inexperienced fliers, they often fly into the wire netting. By decreasing the flying range of the flight the damage to a new fledgling can do to itself is greatly diminished. There is

nothing wrong with this reasoning, except that it is contradictory. The purpose of the flight is to give the birds exercise room, so generally the larger the flight the better. If possible, such bird breeders should use two flight sections of netting padded with nylon instead of wire. Another method greatly used is lining the floor of the flight with foliage. Young birds

This Mexican Red-headed Amazon is a fine example of what a healthy bird looks like. Clear eyes, a well-aligned beak and no discharge coming from the nostrils are all signs of good health.

fly not only to test their wings, but, being nervous, to find a place to hide. This method of lining the floor of the flight works especially well with grass parakeets, which are ground-dwellers.

So vast a topic as the building, design and use of an aviary cannot be fully covered by a book of this size. For those who are

interested in building an aviary from scratch, a book devoted specifically to this subject is recommended. A lot of time and money goes into building an aviary, and this book will go far toward answering any questions on the topic.

PERCHES

Domesticated birds spend a considerable portion of their lives on their perches, and they are really quite important. Birds sometimes copulate on their perches, so they need to be secure. Additionally, perches should be of varying thicknesses so that the birds' feet will not become cramped. In the cage, perches are placed so that birds have enough head room, while in the aviary they are placed near the ceiling for birds to perch in

Your Amazon will require things to stand on that vary in width. Your hand is not a suitable perching item for long periods and therefore other items must be offered for your bird to stand upon.

elevated positions, and spaced far enough apart so that the birds' droppings will not fall into the water dishes or upon the head of other birds.

For Amazon Parrots, perches should vary in thickness from two to four inches, depending upon the species kept. Perches that are too small will not be grasped properly by birds, and if they are too large birds will not be able to maintain their balance.

Both natural branches and purchased perches can be used.

DRINKING FACILITIES

Amazon parrots, unlike the African Grey Parrot, love to bathe. If a single parrot is kept in a wire cage, a mixing bowl might be placed inside from time to time as a treat to allow the bird to get its feathers wet. In the aviary, Amazons would consider it a great treat if the owner would come by with the hose and turn the spray to a fine mist to give them a nice shower. The birds will flap their wings happily and fly around the aviary in a mad rush to get wet. Some bird-owners who have many parrots will install automatic sprinkler systems for the birds' delight on hot, humid days.

The most suitable drinker in an aviary is a clay pie plate or shallow bowl. It should not be so high that the bird has to stand on the lip of the bowl

When two or more birds occupy the same cage it is imperative that you watch each bird's food consumptions and make certain that no one bird is inhibiting the other from eating or drinking.

to drink. A crust of algae will form underneath, which should be scraped away with a putty knife. Some aviarists leave the algae and move the plate so the birds will eat the algae. Algae are rich in iodine; however, the birds will surely step on the growth while eating and that, plus any bacteria that might infest the algae, is good enough reason to scrape it away. Besides, additives like cod-liver oil will provide the iodine that the birds need.

FEEDERS

The selection of the type and number of feeders depends on how many birds are being kept. In a cage, a single bird always has enough feeding compartments to satisfy it. In a large aviary, parrots may take over feeders from the smaller birds. The problem is eliminated by adding enough feeders to go around, but occasionally a single stubborn bird will deny the other birds the right to eat out of spite. In rare cases the bird-owner may have to construct special feeders to cure the bird of this habit.

The size of a feeder should not be so small that the bird exerts itself to feed and not so large that it can stand on the seed as it feeds.

Any natural trees or branches that you allow your Amazon parrot to sit in should be non-toxic and free of pesticides and insecticides.

YOUR AMAZON'S LIFE WITH YOU

THE CAGE

Purchasing an Amazon Parrot is a very big step that requires a lot of consideration. Before any pet is purchased it is wise to give considerable thought to the matter. The Amazon Parrot is best suited to those who spend a lot of time at home, as these birds thrive on companionship. An isolated bird becomes dejected sitting in his cage for

Do not clutter your Amazon's cage too much with toys and playthings. Your parrot would much rather have extra room than a toy hanging in its way.

hours. This usually turns into destructive behavior such as self-mutilation and horrible screeching that the bird owner cannot bear to listen to. The bird is then often doomed to a horrible life of loneliness and is forced to live out the rest of

his days in solitary confinement with only food and water given to him from time to time.

After it has been decided upon that an Amazon Parrot is right for you and your family, the proper type of housing and location of such must be determined before the bird comes to live in your home.

Many prospective Amazon Parrot owners do not realize how large of a cage is actually required for this type of bird. The Amazon itself does not appear to be all that large, however, with his wings fully extended he can be as great as two-and-a-half feet. The Amazon is also an

active bird that must have enough room within his cage to perform all the crazy antics that he may want to do while he is locked within.

The cage itself must be very durable and be able to withstand the Amazon's strong beak. Many cages available at pets stores all over are geared specifically toward the larger parrot's strength and are made to withstand even a Macaw's bite, so there should be no problem in finding a suitable cage. Be certain that the cage you choose is of the stronger gauged barring and that the bars themselves are not placed so far apart that the bird

The bars of the cage you choose should be spaced close enough together so that your Amazon cannot get his head caught in between them.

Amazons are very social birds, and if you do not have the time to spend with your pet, you should get it another Amazon as a friend.

can get his head through them. Likewise, the bars should be coated with a material that is easy to wipe clean and that is non-toxic to your Amazon.

The size of the cage itself will depend on the size Amazon you purchase. The general rule is to allow six inches above the bird's head, six inches below the bird's tail, and three inches on each side of the bird's wings when extended square around the bird. A cage of Two foot square with approximately the same height should suit most species of Amazons just fine.

As already stated, the cage you choose should be easy to clean. The tray on

the bottom should pull out so that droppings and food can be gathered away. Metal trays serve better than plastic ones for the bird s usually do not attempt to chew at the metal, however, plastic will surely be destroyed in no time!

The location of food and water containers is another consideration. While your Amazon parrot might be friendly towards you, he may not like who you choose to mind him while you go on vacation or away for the weekend. The food and water containers must be accessible to this person without him having to put his hands within the cage. Many parrot cages are so designed these days, and a trip your local pet

Your Amazon will appreciate a new and fun toy in his cage from time to time to keep him occupied during the times you are away.

The size cage that you choose for an Amazon Parrot must be large enough so that it may spread its wings without touching the sides of the cage.

store should prove this true.

The cage location is another major consideration. An area in your home that is not drafty, too highly trafficked, or too noisy is usually the best spot for your new friend. Likewise, too much quiet is no good either, otherwise your bird will become frightened at the drop of a hat! The kitchen is not a good place for your bird because fumes from non-stick pans and self-cleaning ovens, as well as the temperature differences that may take place will pose a health hazard for your Amazon.

Never put your bird's cage in front of a sunny

Your Amazon can easily injure itself by sticking his head through the cage bars. To ensure he does not cause harm to himself, do not keep him in a cage where the bar spacing is too far apart.

window, nor in the direct line of a heating or air conditioning vent. The drafts and temperature fluctuations that both of these cause will surely land your Amazon at the veterinarian.

The best location in your home for an Amazon Parrot would be in a corner of your family or living room. Somewhere that sees a lot of activity, however, not a constant hustle and bustle of comings and goings. Corners are best because they reduce the risk of your bird feeling threatened from all cage sides. He can only be approached from the front. Family rooms are also great locations for birds, because they can be included in many family activities, snacks, and restful times. The best

place for your Amazon is definitely where he can feel he is a part of the family.

No fumes, no drafts, no direct sun, plenty of love and attention, your Amazon is on the right road to living a happy life with you!

FREE FLYING

Of course, a caged bird may be permitted free flying time while you or another member of the family is there to supervise it. In fact, all caged birds should have at least one period of free flying every day. Valuable objects should be secured or removed from the flying area. Likewise, anything that can be destroyed by the bird chewing on it should also be removed. Carefully supervise your Amazon while he is out because he will find wood

Never attempt to pick up an unfamiliar Amazon. If aggressive, these birds can take quite a bite!

Domestically bred birds will most likely be hand tame when you purchase them. The Yellow-naped Amazon is one of the more popular species now available on the market.

sprayed lightly with tepid water from a plant mister or other type of spray device. When giving baths, it is best to do so early in the day so that the bird has plenty of time to dry off completely before nightfall and does not become chilled. Some Amazons delight in sharing a shower with their owner, and the pet industry is even picking up on this for they now manufacture specific parrot perches for use within the shower. On a hot summer day, you can even bring your wing clipped Amazon outdoors to delight in a bath with the water hose.

moldings very appealing and they will definitely not withstand the strength of his beak. Houseplants often prove poisonous and should not be in your Amazon's reach. Of course, be aware of open windows and doors while your pet is free flying. Too many pets have been lost from escaping out of these, and it is very difficult to get them back—not to mention life threatening for the bird.

BATHING

In the wild, Amazons love to bathe in the rain. They purposefully expose themselves during a rain shower so that they may enjoy this pleasure. This not only makes them happy, but keeps their feathers in prime condition. Captive birds should be

Your Amazon will enjoy having a shower to keep his plumage clean. Many types of shower perches are commercially available at your local pet shop.

A daily spray with a fine mist will be well enjoyed by your Amazon, and will keep his feathers in great condition too!

BREEDING AMAZON PARROTS

Breeding Amazons in captivity is rare. These parrots are very temperamental and essentially wild birds. Additionally, the price of a breeding pair is a big investment involving hundreds of dollars. Finally, after finding a true pair, the time and patience required may total many years. Amazons are usually sold under a year of age and the hens are not ready to mate until five years of age.

The purpose of this chapter is to familiarize prospective breeders with some of the probelms involved in breeding parrots.

SEXING

Unfortunately, there is no 100 percent fool-proof method of sexing birds using sight alone.

Clues as to the sex of the bird are few. Generally, however, the male is larger than the female and more brightly colored. The head and the beak of the male are noticeably larger. The shape of the eyes is different: the female's are smaller and elliptical in shape, while the male's are more round. Another possible clue is feeling the pelvic bones. The male's pelvic bones are closer together than the female's,

Most Amazons are basically green with other colors on their head and wings. Pictured here is a pair of Green-cheeked Amazons.

because she must pass eggs. Obviously it takes a great deal of familiarity with the species of parrot to make a good guess as to the sex of the bird.

Sexing is critical for breeding, and recently a method has been introduced to determine sex by performing a minor operation on the prospective birds to be bred. A small incision is made in the stomach area. This will not damage the female's ovaries or interfere with the male's sexual reproduction. An operation might seem like an exaggerated way to determine sex, but it isn't considering the difficulty in accurately determining the sex of a bird.

COURTSHIP AND NESTING

The nesting habits of Amazons have rarely been

The courtship and nesting habits of the Amazons is quite romantic. In most Amazon species, the male woos his mate into the nest after he has done a thorough inspection.

A very mature pair of Lilac-crowned Amazons. This species was so named for the obvious lilac patch on its head that extends down to its nape.

observed or described. In captivity, it has been observed that the female takes the lead in courtship and at the onset of breeding will dance around the cock with wings held low and tail spread out. The male, too, may engage in dancing with the feathers displayed. Sometimes, the pupil of the eye dilates. The cock may strut and climb about the

wire. A distinguishing factor of psittacine males is that when they mount the female they always place both feet on the back. Just before copulation there will be considerable body contact according to Foreshaw in his book *Parrots of the World.*

Many Amazon species can only be saved by captive breeding programs. Too many habitats have been destroyed through deforestation and much of the food supply that these birds thrive on has disappeared.

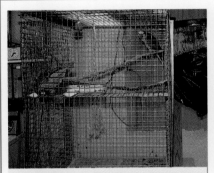

A breeding pair of Amazons will require a roomy flight, adequate lighting, and a large nest box in order to be successful.

Parrots are notorious for their lack of selection of a suitable nesting site in the aviary. Often the hen will lay her eggs on the floor of the cage and incubate them there. She will become distraught if any attempts are made to induce her to incubate her eggs in a nest box.

For breeding purposes a nest box should be placed in the cage. It should be made of sturdy wood and lined with a smaller layer of peat. Since Amazons prefer tree hollows, the inside of the nest box should not allow much light inside and should not be too spacious. Once the hen lays, the nest should not be disturbed. Incubation is approximately 28 days. The male will feed the female, who in turn will feed the young regurgitated food.

Egg problems are usually associated with deficiencies of grit and greens in the diet. The formation of the egg shell in the hen is greatly dependent on the diet of the bird. The shell must be of porous nature to allow oxygen and carbon dioxide to pass freely to the developing embryo, and also hard enough to serve as a layer of protection. Deficiencies of calcium are responsible for egg-binding and soft-shelled eggs.

Egg-bound is a condition whereby the hen is unable to expel her eggs; they become stuck in the pelvic area, and if not removed both hen and egg will die. The hen will usually try vainly to expel the egg and paralysis may occur. This condition can be diagnosed by feeling for the egg in the stomach region.

Egg-binding is often associated with a lack of calcium, but the condition may occur in old hens. Some bird-owners can free the egg by inserting a well oiled finger into the cloaca and up into the oviduct. By gentle pressure with the free hand on the stomach they can expel the egg. This is a delicate operation, for if the egg breaks the hen may die. If the bird is to be saved at all, however, action must be taken very soon after the condition is diagnosed, otherwise the bird will die. A soft-shelled egg is usually caused by a calcium deficiency.

Be certain that the Amazon parrots you pair together are indeed a pair. Verification cannot be made by sight and therefore a veterinary exam and probably a blood test will need to be performed.

DISEASE

Amazons are, on the whole, healthy birds. If they do contract a disease they will not quickly succumb to it. Most reliable bird establishments will guarantee the health of their stock. It is a good idea to take your parrot to the veterinarian within 24 hours of bringing him home to verify his health. The parrot that you buy in the pet shop is usually a very healthy bird.

The best advice ever given to the owner of a sick bird is to take it to a veterinarian immediately. This is especially pertinent for the aviary owner, where a contagious disease could wipe out his entire stock of exotic birds. Even if the bird dies overnight it should be taken to a veterinarian, who will do a post-mortem on the bird to discover the reason it died. This is sometimes called "posting."

The subject of bird diseases is a large one. The purpose of this chapter is to identify some of the more common bird ailments along with recommended care. As a more complete reference see *Bird Diseases* by L. Arnall and I.F. Keymer.

IDENTIFYING A SICK BIRD

Sick birds are not so easily identified. In the case of Amazons, a bird may be healthy one day and dead the next. There are some general symptoms, however, which usually take the form of a change of habits. They may refuse to fly and sit in a corner of the cage. Another common symptom is that the bird has its feathers fluffed up. This is a sign that the bird is trying to retain its body heat by using dead air spaces under its feathers as insulation.

Runny droppings may indicate illness or they may not indicate illness at all, since they may be caused by a change in diet. Diarrhea is not a disease but a symptom, and the bird should be removed to a hospital cage to see if the condition will clear up.

Other general symptoms are: irregular breathing; the tail jerking up and down; and eyes that are continually closed or discharging fluid.

Any of the mentioned symptoms indicate a bird that is sick, and it should be immediately removed to a hospital cage and taken to a veterinarian as soon as possible.

COLDS

Colds are the most common ailment that a bird will get. They are caused by viruses and are similar to the colds humans catch. The symptoms for a cold are runny nose, sneezing and coughing. While a cold itself is not so serious, left unattended it may develop into pneumonia.

The bird should be removed to a hospital cage with a temperature setting of 95°F. If the eyes are running, epsom salts added to mineral water should be offered.

DIARRHEA

Diarrhea can be a symptom of many diseases. At the same time, diarrhea can persist for a long time without any other effects. Diarrhea is really the result of an inflammation of the intestines or cloaca with the secretion of an abnormal amount of fluid in the droppings, that become soft and watery. Because of the acid nature of the droppings the tissues surrounding the vent become inflamed.

Placing the bird in a hospital cage is not necessary since the bird, unless it has contracted a major disease, has no fever. If the condition does not clear up, the bird should be taken to a veterinarian. Check to see if a change in diet has not caused this condition.

It is often stated that green food should be discontinued; in fact some authorities have stated that if the bird's droppings contain blood, it may be caused by greens.

In any case, if persistent, diarrhea may indicate a variety of ailments; a tumor in the kidney, liver damage, inflammation of the urinary tract and a variety of bacterial infections.

PREMATURE MOLT

Premature molt is not strictly speaking a disease; it is a nervous habit, often called displacement preening. Its symptoms are an excessive picking of the feathers by the bird and scratching the head and feet to excess. In premature molt the bird will do this to such a degree that healthy feathers will be pulled out, leaving bald patches.

Since premature molt is not a disease but a nervous habit, it is difficult to diagnose. For one thing, all birds preen and, in the case of parrots, preening is quite vigorous. Also, birds molt at least once a year (every eight months for Amazons), and it is normal for them to scratch excessively as the new pinfeathers break the surface of the skin.

Premature molt is rarely lethal, but in extreme cases, where the bird is picking itself bald, there is really no cure. It is caused by the bird's isolation and ill-feelings over confinement. Perhaps the best treatment is to install toys inside the cage in the hope the that bird will occupy itself with these rather than pick at its feathers.

BROKEN LIMBS

Broken wings are common enough and merely need to be set. In some cases the wing will have to be removed. This should be done by a veterinarian since he will be using a sterilized instrument. Some birdmen can set the limb using a match or blade of wood, but this requires experience since if improperly set it will not heal correctly. The wing is set in a flexed position, and the owner should provide perches near the ground for these birds.

A broken leg should also be set by a veterinarian. Properly set the bird will not be immobilized.

MITES

So many kinds of mites attack birds that it is difficult to find a comprehensive list and treatment. Mites attack the feathers, the skin, the air sacs, the feet, etc. This section will be concerned with two mites:one that causes scaly-leg and a common blood-sucking mite known as the red mite.

Scaly-leg is caused by a very tiny mite that bores under the scales of the feet and lives on the connective tissue. Scaly-leg can be diagnosed in birds whose feet have unduly large scales a consequently dirty appearance to the legs. The mite that causes this ailment is less than 1/200th of an inch long and almost impossible to see without the aid of a magnifying glass.

The introduction of this mite into an aviary is caused by using unclean perches, failing to wash the perches when they become dirty or introducing birds into the aviary without washing their feet.

The cure is simple enough. First, all the perches should be cleaned. Then the bird's feet should be washed with olive oil to soften the scaly appearance. After a few days these scales can be taken off without harm and the tissue underneath anointed with either olive oil or petroleum jelly. The oil or jelly will suffocate the mites.

The red mite (*Dermanyssus*) is seen quite frequently. It is a small tick-like creature which measures about 1/75 to 1/100th of an inch in length. By gently separating the bird's feathers, these mites can be spotted.

The red mite gets is name because, being a blood-sucker at night, it will be gorged with blood the following day and if crushed will become a red splotch from the blood. Red mites attack only at night and during the day seek some shelter to hide in, usually the cracks of the perches, nests and the aviary. Among breeders, they can become so numerous as to drive the hen from her nest and bleed the young chicks to death.

Since red mites leave the birds during the day, they can be spotted and killed. The general remedy is to completely cleanse the aviary, washing or even replacing the perches, and washing and spraying with a safe insecticide the rest of the aviary. Straw used in next-boxes should be removed.

TAPEWORMS

Contrary to popular belief, there are quite a few species of tapeworms. There are at least nine species of tapeworms that attack chickens and turkeys. Diagnosis is that the feces will contain worm segments in the droppings; the droppings are at first watery, but later brownish yellow due to bleeding.

An infestation of tapeworm in a well-run aviary is rare because it requires an infected bird getting into the aviary. Tapeworms attach themselves to the mucous membranes of the intestines and release their eggs into the feces of the bird; if these feces are digested by another bird then that bird will become infected.

Tapeworms luckily are rarely fatal, and once

diagnosed there are a number of medications that will wipe them out.

ROUNDWORMS

Like tapeworms, there are many varieties of roundworms. They range in size according to the size of the bird. Those found in canaries are from one-quarter to three-quarters of an inch long.

These worms are passed on through the feces and through the food. They are very dangerous since they multiply to such numbers that they may block the intestines and kill the bird. They can be diagnosed in the feces, but only under a microscope. The best cure is prevention: keep the cage clean on a regular basis.

Feather plucking is a bad habit that many birds fall victim to. This Yellow-fronted Amazon is wearing a collar designed so that he cannot pick at his feathers.

SUGGESTED READING

PS-753

Parrots of the World

by J.M. Forshaw
Almost 500 species and subspecies are presented here. 584 pages, over 300 full-color plates.

TS-242

Training Captive–Bred Parrots

by Delia Berlin
Most of the parrots sold today were bred in captivity and hand reared. They are much easier to handle, tame and train than wild-caught birds. This book tells and shows parrot owners how to take advantage of that important feature.

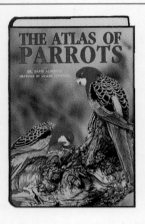

H-1109

Atlas of Parrots

by David Alderton, Illustrations by G. Stevenson
Illustrated coverage of every species and and subspecies of parrot in the world. 544 pages, over 300 full-color plates.

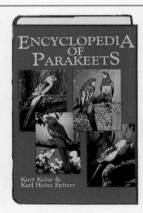

H-1094

Encyclopedia of Parakeets

by K. Kolar and K.H. Spitzer
This thorough coverage ranges from little known species to the familiar budgerigar and cockatiel. 223 pages with many full-color photos.

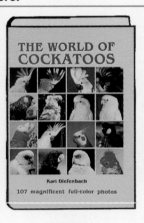

H-1072

The World of Cockatoos

by Karl Diefenbach
A highly informative book detailing everything the Cockatoo lover needs to know. 208 pages, 80 full-color photos.

H-1055

World of Amazon Parrots

Encyclopedia of Amazon Parrots a complete file of color photos and range maps makes for easy identification with specifics on species and subspecies. Illustrated with full-color photos and range maps.